PRAYING IN THE SPIRIT OF
CATHERINE McAULEY

A COLLECTION OF PRAYERS

WRITTEN OR COMPILED BY

THE SISTERS OF MERCY OF THE AMERICAS

PRAYING IN THE SPIRIT OF
CATHERINE McAULEY

ACKNOWLEDGMENTS

Special gratitude is due to Margaret Brault, RSM, for her
careful preparation of the manuscript, to Mary Sullivan,
RSM, for her special assistance throughout the project,
and to the staff of Liturgy Training Publications for their
able assistance in the design and production of this book.

The sculpture of Catherine McAuley depicted on
the cover of this book is by Marie Henderson, RSM.
Photograph by Julie May. This book was designed
by Lisa Buckley and set in type by Mark Hollopeter.
Calligraphy by Rosie Kelly.

CONTENTS

CATHERINE MCAULEY was born in Dublin, Ireland, in 1778. Her father died when she was five. After her mother died in 1798, she lived with relatives until she moved in with the Callaghans, an elderly couple whom she cared for until their deaths. With the inheritance she received from them, she founded the House of Mercy on Baggot Street, Dublin, in 1827 to provide shelter for homeless servant girls and women, education for poor children and visitation of the sick poor in their homes and in hospitals. Catherine founded the Sisters of Mercy in 1831 to continue these works of mercy. She died ten years later, in November 1841. Today Sisters of Mercy, with their associates and co-workers, minister throughout the world wherever need calls and their resources permit.

INTRODUCTION

In her *Retreat Instructions,* Catherine McAuley reminded the newly founded Sisters of Mercy that "our center is God, from whom all our actions should spring as from their source" (p. 154) and therefore "our whole life should be a continual act of praise and prayer" (p. 44). From the beginning of the Institute, we have centered ourselves in God and deepened our commitment to the works of mercy through the daily practice of personal and communal prayer.

This volume, *Praying in the Spirit of Catherine McAuley,* invites its users to enter into the spirit of faith and compassion characteristic of the prayer of Catherine and her daughters. The following is a description of its contents, a blend of traditional prayers, contemporary adaptations and historical texts.

Part One: "Prayers Inspired by the Prayer of Catherine McAuley" presents, in contemporary idiom and theological understanding, prayers that Catherine either composed or cherished. Some, like the Psalter of Jesus, were part of her daily prayer from her earliest years; others were an expression of her deepening surrender to God's action and love for her. Just as these prayers in their original form shaped Catherine's own heart of mercy, so one hopes that they will help to form the prayer of Mercy today.

Part Two: "Prayers in the Mercy Spirit" contains a variety of prayers marking special moments in the life of Mercy. These prayers were either specifically composed for this collection or drawn from prayers that have long been part of our Mercy tradition.

Part Three: "Rituals Marking the Death of a Sister" — one of the great sorrows of Catherine McAuley's life was the death of so many members of the early Mercy community. In a letter to Sister Mary Teresa White, she remarks, "The tomb seems never closed in my regard." It was during times of loss that Catherine and the community experienced the deepest bonds of hope and union. This volume provides three contemporary rituals that are meant to supplement the rituals provided in the *Order of Christian Funerals.* Each ritual may be used as designed or adapted to suit local circumstances.

Part Four: "The Prayers of Catherine McAuley" presents the original texts of prayers that Catherine herself composed or that she frequently prayed. These prayers, assembled, introduced and annotated by Sister Mary Sullivan, RSM, are provided for use in personal prayer or in research. Reflection on these prayers helps us to enter into the mind and heart of Catherine and of the early Mercy women who carried her legacy throughout the world.

May all those who pray these prayers be touched by the Spirit of Mercy that animated Catherine McAuley. May they grow fearless in faith, generous in love and rich in mercy.

The Editorial Committee
Sister Virginia Mary Andrews, RSM
Sister Mary Jo Baldus, RSM
Sister Sheila Carney, RSM
Sister Katherine Doyle, RSM
Sister Doris Gottemoeller, RSM
Sister Alice Swartz, RSM

PART ONE

Prayers Inspired
by the Prayer
of Catherine McAuley

SUSCIPE OF CATHERINE MCAULEY

MY GOD, I am yours for time and eternity. Teach me to cast myself entirely into the arms of your loving providence with the most lively, unlimited confidence in your compassionate, tender pity. Grant me, O most merciful Redeemer, that whatever you ordain or permit may be acceptable to me. Take from my heart all painful anxiety; suffer nothing to sadden me but sin; nothing to delight me but the hope of coming to the possession of you, my God and my all, in your everlasting kingdom. Amen.

MORNING OFFERING

O COMPASSIONATE Jesus, look on me today with tenderness and give me the grace to walk on the path of mercy marked out for those who follow you. May all that I do today reflect your merciful love. Amen.

PRAYER FOR A SISTER CRITICALLY ILL

HEALING GOD, give strength and courage to our sister (N._____) as she patiently endures the suffering and pain of her illness. Take from her heart all painful anxiety. Help her to place herself in the arms of your loving providence, trusting in your compassionate, tender love.

Blessed Mary and all the saints, gather round us as we pray for our sister. May we reach out to her with compassion and support, bringing her comfort. Through your intercession may we all look forward to being united with you in God's presence. Amen.

A PRAYER FOR THOSE WHO ARE POOR

MY GOD, look with compassion and mercy on those who are poor, and grant us grace to do all that we can for their relief and comfort. We ask your blessing this day — in the name and for the sake of our Lord and Savior, Jesus Christ. Amen.

PRAYER BEFORE MEDITATION

COME HOLY Spirit, dwell in our hearts and kindle in them the fire of your divine love.

O eternal God, grant to us, we beseech you, the fullness of your divine Spirit and give us openness to the inspirations of your grace. Help us to put aside every thought and concern that may distract us from your holy presence. Through the life and death of Jesus Christ and through the intercession of Mary and all the saints, we sincerely ask that this prayer may glorify you and bring us to salvation. Amen.

ACT OF CONSECRATION

GOD OF my heart, my whole desire is in loving you. I give myself to you without reserve.

I consecrate to you my heart. Receive it as an offering of love and unite it to your heart. I desire to dwell with you all my days.

I consecrate to you my will. May it be joined to yours in all things. May my deepest desire be to do what is pleasing to you. May your Spirit guide me in the way of obedience, and may selfish desires not find a home in me.

I consecrate to you my understanding. May I see with your eyes and choose what is life giving. May I forgo all that is false and passing, that I may embrace what is true and enduring. Let me desire the good and all that brings the good to birth. May your grace bring my desire to realization.

I consecrate to you my memory. Let me always remember your goodness and beauty. I shall take delight in remembering your favors — the love and mercy you have shown to me. May my heart be ever grateful.

I consecrate to you my body. Make me a worthy dwelling for your Spirit. Jesus, I give you all that I am, and I accept whatever limitations, sickness, sorrows and death will be mine. Let me desire what you desire. No matter how painful the cross that is mine to carry, I receive it with confidence in your strength and grace. May I accept it with lively gratitude, and carry it with joy and constancy. May the words of St. Paul strengthen me: "With Christ I am nailed to the cross."

I consecrate to you all that I may ever possess in goods, influence, or status. All is yours. Do with me what you will. I consecrate to you all that I can — joys, sorrows, life and death — to offer you my love and to witness to others the joy of loving you. May I serve you with devotion, relying on the help of your grace. May I be yours without reserve until the last moment of my life. Amen.

THIRTY DAYS' PRAYER

It was Catherine McAuley's custom to pray the two Thirty Days' Prayers in times of need, at the establishment of new foundations and for benefactors and co-workers. The following adaptation combines themes from the Thirty Days' Prayer to Jesus Christ the Redeemer and the Thirty Days' Prayer to the Blessed Virgin Mary.

~

MERCIFUL JESUS, you inspired in Catherine McAuley a lively conviction of your enduring love. In times of need she and her companions faithfully entreated your help, and they were never disappointed. In this same confident spirit we come to you now.

Because you walked among us, you know our human experience. You have shared our joys and sorrows. You have healed and comforted us, sustained and renewed us. Be with us now in this time of need. Let us experience your loving presence as you grant this favor we ask of you: _____.

We also ask your blessing on our living and deceased family members, our sisters in community, our associates and benefactors. Show them your loving kindness.

Encouraged by your care for us, we will, with lively fidelity, devote ourselves to the works of mercy. Through our good works, may your people experience your unceasing care for them. We ask all this through the intercession of Mary, your mother and our mother of Mercy.

THE PSALTER OF JESUS

From her earliest years Catherine McAuley prayed the Psalter of Jesus. Fifteen petitions asking for the mercy and compassion of God composed the general format of the prayer. Each petition invoked the name of Jesus ten times. From this pattern evolved the title of the Psalter, for the petitioner invoked the name of Jesus 150 times, paralleling the 150 psalms of the biblical Psalter. The intent of the Psalter of Jesus was to honor the person, name and mission of Jesus and to plead for the saving love and guidance made possible by Jesus' death and resurrection.

The following prayer is an adaptation of the Psalter of Jesus that Catherine prayed. It is inspired by her trust in God's mercy and her constant intercession for those in need, as well as by her devotion to the example of Jesus. Those who pray this adapted form of the Psalter are free to use the elements of the prayer in whatever ways will most enkindle their reverence and zeal.

~

At the name of Jesus every knee should bend, in heaven and on earth and under the earth, and every tongue should confess that Jesus Christ is Lord, to the glory of God the Father.
Philippians 2:10 – 11

Jesus, have mercy on me and forgive the wrong I have done in
your sight. Do not hold against me my ingratitude for the
mercies you have shown to me.

Have pity on me, *Jesus,* for I am weak and in need of healing.
Help me, for I am unable to help myself.

Jesus, never let me put success, pleasure, comfort or security
before your love, but let me always hold you first in
my heart.

Jesus, compassionate one, trusting in your love, I ask that you
have mercy on your suffering people.

Jesus, liberator and redeemer, set free those who are held captive
by sin and injustice and heal the wounds caused by sin.

Where there is division in families, communities and nations,
Jesus, bring unity.

Where war and violence stalk the land, *Jesus,* bring peace and
understanding.

Jesus, make my heart like yours and use me to witness to others
the reality of your saving love.

Jesus, have mercy on all who wander from you. Through
your mercy make us sincere lovers of you and faithful
followers of your gospel. Transform our sins and failings
into virtues and give us joy in loving you. *Jesus,* through
your passion, death and resurrection and for the sake
of your name, have mercy on our sisters and brothers who
have died and bring them home to dwell with you in glory.
O Blessed Trinity, one eternal God, have mercy on us.

SECOND PETITION: *Jesus, come to me in my need.*

Jesus, you are my protector and shelter in time of trial. Help
me to resist the lure of temptation and devote myself to the
practice of virtue.

Jesus, in your mercy, remove from my heart any longing for
comfort, pleasure or security that may lead me to the way
of self-indulgence.

Strengthen me, *Jesus,* to live a just and peaceable life.

Jesus, you laid down your life for me. Give me the power to deny myself whatever may keep me from loving you.

Jesus, compassionate one, trusting in your love, I ask that you have mercy on your suffering people.

Heed the cries of those who have no food or shelter, *Jesus,* and send them relief.

Jesus, open the hearts of all peoples to share the gifts of the earth with those who lack what is needed to sustain life.

Jesus, make my heart like yours and use me to witness to others the reality of your saving love.

Jesus, have mercy on all who wander from you. Through your mercy make us sincere lovers of you and faithful followers of your gospel. Transform our sins and failings into virtues and give us joy in loving you. *Jesus,* through your passion, death and resurrection and for the sake of your name, have mercy on our sisters and brothers who have died and bring them home to dwell with you in glory. O Blessed Trinity, one eternal God, have mercy on us.

THIRD PETITION: *Jesus, strengthen me to follow you.*

Jesus, strengthen me that I may follow you in fidelity and love.

May I praise you, *Jesus,* in my words and actions, and may you bring me and those whom I serve to everlasting joy.

Jesus, let the works of my hands bring healing and justice to your people, and hope to those who await your coming.

Jesus, I am a fragile vessel containing your glory. Grant me conversion of heart that I may change what is unloving in my life, strive to live the Gospel message more faithfully, and repair the harm I have caused others.

Jesus, compassionate one, trusting in your love, I ask that you have mercy on your suffering people.

Hear the cries of the forgotten ones in our society, *Jesus,* and let them know the healing power of your mercy.

Jesus, comfort the children who never feel the warmth of
an embrace; sustain with your presence those who feel
the pain of isolation and rejection.

Jesus, make my heart like yours and use me to witness to others
the reality of your saving love.

Jesus, have mercy on all who wander from you. Through
your mercy make us sincere lovers of you and faithful
followers of your gospel. Transform our sins and failings
into virtues and give us joy in loving you. *Jesus,* through
your passion, death and resurrection and for the sake
of your name, have mercy on our sisters and brothers who
have died and bring them home to dwell with you in glory.
O Blessed Trinity, one eternal God, have mercy on us.

FOURTH PETITION: *Jesus, heal the emptiness of my heart.*

Jesus, comfort me in times of loneliness. Let the emptiness of
my heart be filled by your presence.

Jesus, let me find my joy in loving you. Give me the gift of your
longing to quicken my devotion, *Jesus,* and your light to
illumine my prayer.

Jesus, let me welcome the restlessness that leads me to you; may
I fix my gaze upon you.

Jesus, compassionate one, trusting in your love, I ask that you
have mercy on your suffering people.

Jesus, send those who search for meaning in their lives, the gift
of your Spirit.

Jesus, fill their emptiness with your abiding companionship.

Open the eyes of the lonely and alienated to your presence,
Jesus. May they know that you call them friends.

Jesus, make my heart like yours and use me to witness to others
the reality of your saving love.

Jesus, have mercy on all who wander from you. Through
your mercy make us sincere lovers of you and faithful
followers of your gospel. Transform our sins and failings
into virtues and give us joy in loving you. *Jesus,* through

your passion, death and resurrection and for the sake
of your name, have mercy on our sisters and brothers who
have died and bring them home to dwell with you in glory.
O Blessed Trinity, one eternal God, have mercy on us.

FIFTH PETITION: *Jesus, make firm my feet upon life's way.*

Jesus, make me steadfast in faith, hope and love; direct my feet
in the way of your justice.

Jesus, let me never forget that I follow you, my crucified
Savior. Through your sufferings, I have been given life
and wholeness.

Increase my patience in times of trial, *Jesus,* and fortify my
spirit in times of tribulation.

Jesus, let me rely on your providence even in the midst of doubt
and discouragement.

Jesus, compassionate one, trusting in your love, I ask that you
have mercy on your suffering people.

I ask you, *Jesus,* to strengthen and comfort all those who suffer
persecution for your sake.

Jesus, be with them in their night of suffering; give them
courage to speak the word of truth.

Jesus, make my heart like yours and use me to witness to others
the reality of your saving love.

Jesus, have mercy on all who wander from you. Through
your mercy make us sincere lovers of you and faithful
followers of your gospel. Transform our sins and failings
into virtues and give us joy in loving you. *Jesus,* through
your passion, death and resurrection and for the sake
of your name, have mercy on our sisters and brothers who
have died and bring them home to dwell with you in glory.
O Blessed Trinity, one eternal God, have mercy on us.

SIXTH PETITION: *Jesus, fill me with wisdom so I may know your love.*

Jesus, fill me with wisdom so that I may know you; illumine my
    understanding that I may recognize the good and pursue it.
Give me courage, *Jesus,* to live in a way that will glorify you.
May my life, *Jesus,* be a witness to the faltering, and my words
    counsel for the disheartened.
Jesus, compassionate one, trusting in your love, I ask that you
    have mercy on your suffering people.
Send your Spirit of wisdom, *Jesus,* to guide the decisions of our
    religious and civil leaders. Stir up in them the determination
    to serve the common good.
When choices that bring life or death are set before us, give us,
    Jesus, the wisdom to choose life.
Jesus, inspire all leaders to live lives of integrity and justice and
    to serve those who are most in need.
Jesus, make my heart like yours and use me to witness to others
    the reality of your saving love.
Jesus, have mercy on all who wander from you. Through
    your mercy make us sincere lovers of you and faithful
    followers of your gospel. Transform our sins and failings
    into virtues and give us joy in loving you. *Jesus,* through
    your passion, death and resurrection and for the sake
    of your name, have mercy on our sisters and brothers who
    have died and bring them home to dwell with you in glory.
    O Blessed Trinity, one eternal God, have mercy on us.

SEVENTH PETITION: *Jesus, let me fear nothing but the loss of you.*

Jesus, let me treasure you more than life itself. Fill me with
    longing love.
Jesus, in the big and small choices of each day, let me always
    choose what is pleasing to you.
Animate my heart, *Jesus,* with an ardent zeal that I may never
    weary of doing good.

In the midst of struggle and uncertainty, let me remember, *Jesus,*
that you are my strength and my salvation. You are the
one in whom I hope.

Jesus, compassionate one, trusting in your love, I ask that you
have mercy on your suffering people.

In your mercy, *Jesus,* give the gift of perseverance to those who
struggle to be faithful to the way of discipleship.

Jesus, keep the lure of fortune, power, or security from obscuring
the truth that you are our greatest treasure.

Jesus, make my heart like yours and use me to witness to others
the reality of your saving love.

Jesus, have mercy on all who wander from you. Through
your mercy make us sincere lovers of you and faithful
followers of your gospel. Transform our sins and failings
into virtues and give us joy in loving you. *Jesus,* through
your passion, death and resurrection and for the sake
of your name, have mercy on our sisters and brothers who
have died and bring them home to dwell with you in glory.
O Blessed Trinity, one eternal God, have mercy on us.

EIGHTH PETITION: *Jesus, grant me the grace to love you.*

Jesus, grant me the grace to love you who are loving and
compassionate.

Jesus, let me give thanks for your goodness and kindness to me,
for the bounty bestowed upon me day after day.

What you have done for me and for your people, loving *Jesus,*
do for us always.

Jesus, may my whole being yearn for you; give me your strength,
that I may follow where you lead me.

Jesus, compassionate one, trusting in your love, I ask that you
have mercy on your suffering people.

Let the remembrance of your kindness and patience, *Jesus,*
overcome our hardness of heart and keep us from deeds
of darkness.

Jesus, you have rescued us from dangers and filled our spirits
with the consolations of your word and presence. In your
mercy sustain your disciples in the difficult passages of
their journey and lead them to everlasting joy.

Jesus, make my heart like yours and use me to witness to others
the reality of your saving love.

Jesus, have mercy on all who wander from you. Through
your mercy make us sincere lovers of you and faithful
followers of your gospel. Transform our sins and failings
into virtues and give us joy in loving you. *Jesus,* through
your passion, death and resurrection and for the sake
of your name, have mercy on our sisters and brothers who
have died and bring them home to dwell with you in glory.
O Blessed Trinity, one eternal God, have mercy on us.

NINTH PETITION: *Jesus, strengthen me to welcome death
as your visitation.*

Jesus, grant me the grace to welcome death as your visitation.
Let it not come to me as a fearful stranger, but as a gentle
invitation to come home to you.

Jesus, in the hour of my death may I be comforted by the
presence of Mary and all the saints of God.

Defend me, *Jesus,* against the fear and doubt of that hour. Fill
me with peace and hope in your promise of abiding life.

Jesus, compassionate one, trusting in your love, I ask that you
have mercy on your suffering people.

Do not abandon those who are dying, *Jesus,* but sustain them
against the uncertainties of that experience.

Jesus, pour your grace on our dying brothers and sisters that
they may embrace all people in forgiveness and love.

Jesus, prepare us for our death by helping us to die to self. In
our daily dying and rising, bring us to conversion of heart.

Jesus, make my heart like yours and use me to witness to others
the reality of your saving love.

Jesus, have mercy on all who wander from you. Through
your mercy make us sincere lovers of you and faithful
followers of your gospel. Transform our sins and failings
into virtues and give us joy in loving you. *Jesus,* through
your passion, death and resurrection and for the sake
of your name, have mercy on our sisters and brothers who
have died and bring them home to dwell with you in glory.
O Blessed Trinity, one eternal God, have mercy on us.

TENTH PETITION: *Jesus, let me embrace the transforming crosses
of my life.*

Jesus, let me use the trials and crosses of today to purify my heart.
Like gold tried in the furnace, *Jesus,* may I be fired in the furnace
of my daily service.
Jesus, let me not seek to escape the refining challenges and
difficulties of my life, but rather embrace them with love.
Strengthen me to accept those crosses and afflictions that you
know, *Jesus,* will enkindle in me a deeper love for you.
Jesus, compassionate one, trusting in your love, I ask that you
have mercy on your suffering people.
Give those who meet suffering in the form of poverty, margin-
alization or oppression the vision to know that it is with
you, *Jesus,* that they are nailed to the cross. Let them know
that they are not alone in their sufferings.
Give us humble hearts, *Jesus,* purified by the fire of your love
so that at life's end we may come home to you in whom we
live, move and have our being.
Jesus, make my heart like yours and use me to witness to others
the reality of your saving love.
Jesus, have mercy on all who wander from you. Through
your mercy make us sincere lovers of you and faithful
followers of your gospel. Transform our sins and failings
into virtues and give us joy in loving you. *Jesus,* through
your passion, death and resurrection and for the sake

of your name, have mercy on our sisters and brothers who
have died and bring them home to dwell with you in glory.
O Blessed Trinity, one eternal God, have mercy on us.

ELEVENTH PETITION: *Jesus, help me to see you in your people
who are poor.*

Jesus, you who are the lover of the poor, make my heart
compassionate and merciful.

May I see you, *Jesus,* in the stranger and the outcast, in the
homeless and the hungry.

Jesus, expand my heart that I may long to share what I have
with those who have less.

May I open my heart in hospitality, *Jesus,* welcoming each guest
as yourself.

Jesus, compassionate one, trusting in your love, I ask that you
have mercy on your suffering people.

Hasten the day, *Jesus,* when no one will know the pain of
powerlessness or alienation.

Jesus, although our world is filled with invitations to root
ourselves in material possessions and passing pleasures and
successes, may we know that only your love is enduring.

Jesus, make my heart like yours and use me to witness to others
the reality of your saving love.

Jesus, have mercy on all who wander from you. Through
your mercy make us sincere lovers of you and faithful
followers of your gospel. Transform our sins and failings
into virtues and give us joy in loving you. *Jesus,* through
your passion, death and resurrection and for the sake
of your name, have mercy on our sisters and brothers who
have died and bring them home to dwell with you in glory.
O Blessed Trinity, one eternal God, have mercy on us.

TWELFTH PETITION: *Jesus, teach me to trust in your loving help.*

Jesus, in all my necessities, teach me to call on you for help.

Jesus, you answered the prayer of the widow of Nain and heard
the pleas of Bartimaeus, the blind beggar. At the moment
of my need, hear me too.

I trust in you, *Jesus,* as a child trusts in her mother, knowing
that you know my needs before they spring from my lips.

Turn my heart to your desire, *Jesus,* that my intercessions may
be in harmony with your own heart. Confident that your
mercy will bring life, I ask that you _____.

Jesus, compassionate one, trusting in your love, I ask that you
have mercy on your suffering people.

Jesus, you promised us: "Ask and you shall receive; seek and
you shall find; knock and the door shall be opened to you."
Will you deliver us, O Saving One?

Heal the brokenness of our world, *Jesus,* and fill the earth with
the blessedness of peace.

Jesus, make my heart like yours and use me to witness to others
the reality of your saving love.

Jesus, have mercy on all who wander from you. Through
your mercy make us sincere lovers of you and faithful
followers of your gospel. Transform our sins and failings
into virtues and give us joy in loving you. *Jesus,* through
your passion, death and resurrection and for the sake
of your name, have mercy on our sisters and brothers who
have died and bring them home to dwell with you in glory.
O Blessed Trinity, one eternal God, have mercy on us.

THIRTEENTH PETITION: *Jesus, help me to persevere in holiness.*

Jesus, help me to persevere in virtue and in a holy life.

Grant that I may never grow weary of doing good, *Jesus,*
or cease my labors until your reign of justice flourishes
throughout the earth.

In the observance of our Constitutions and in the performance
of my duties, *Jesus,* let my spirit be animated by love.

Jesus, what is my life but a pilgrimage home to you? Let me
not lose my way or slacken the journey.

Jesus, compassionate one, trusting in your love, I ask that you
have mercy on your suffering people.

Jesus, keep ever before our minds the model of your life and
death. Let all who are called to the life of Mercy remember
the passion and suffering you embraced for us, for without
your cross there is no crown.

Jesus, etch in our hearts your words: "The one who perseveres
to the end shall be saved."

Jesus, make my heart like yours and use me to witness to others
the reality of your saving love.

Jesus, have mercy on all who wander from you. Through
your mercy make us sincere lovers of you and faithful
followers of your gospel. Transform our sins and failings
into virtues and give us joy in loving you. *Jesus,* through
your passion, death and resurrection and for the sake
of your name, have mercy on our sisters and brothers who
have died and bring them home to dwell with you in glory.
O Blessed Trinity, one eternal God, have mercy on us.

FOURTEENTH PETITION: *Jesus, let me fix my gaze on you.*

Jesus, grant me constancy to fix my mind on you in my prayer,
in my work, in all the activities of my day.

Arrest my wandering thoughts, *Jesus,* and calm the waters of
distraction and fatigue. Loosen the bonds of those attach-
ments that keep me from being centered in you.

When I cannot find the words with which to pray, *Jesus,* may
your Spirit pray in me.

When my eyes fail to see those around me as you see them,
Jesus, flood my vision with your light.

Jesus, compassionate one, trusting in your love, I ask that you
have mercy on your suffering people.

Jesus, in the darkness of uncertainty be light for those who
   search for you.
Attach our hearts to you, *Jesus,* and empower us to love you
   more dearly and follow you more faithfully.
Jesus, make my heart like yours and use me to witness to others
   the reality of your saving love.
Jesus, have mercy on all who wander from you. Through
   your mercy make us sincere lovers of you and faithful
   followers of your gospel. Transform our sins and failings
   into virtues and give us joy in loving you. *Jesus,* through
   your passion, death and resurrection and for the sake
   of your name, have mercy on our sisters and brothers who
   have died and bring them home to dwell with you in glory.
   O Blessed Trinity, one eternal God, have mercy on us.

FIFTEENTH PETITION: *Jesus, into your hands I place my life.*

Jesus, grant me the grace to surrender my life into your hands,
   to employ every faculty of soul and body in the service
   of your will.
Let the love and service of my life bring others closer to you,
   Jesus, and may my only desire be longing to dwell in you.
Soften the hardness of my heart, *Jesus,* and melt my haughtiness
   into obedient humility.
At the hour of my death, *Jesus,* let me release my spirit into
   your hands.
Jesus, compassionate one, trusting in your love, I ask that you
   have mercy on your suffering people.
May the remembrance of your passion strengthen us, *Jesus,*
   to endure all trials and sufferings for your love.
Help us to remember, *Jesus,* that whatever we gain is lost if
   we lose you; whatever we lose is nothing compared to
   your love.
Jesus, make my heart like yours and use me to witness to others
   the reality of your saving love, all the days of my life.

Jesus, have mercy on all who wander from you. Through
your mercy make us sincere lovers of you and faithful
followers of your gospel. Transform our sins and failings
into virtues and give us joy in loving you. *Jesus,* through
your passion, death and resurrection and for the sake
of your name, have mercy on our sisters and brothers who
have died and bring them home to dwell with you in glory.
O Blessed Trinity, one eternal God, have mercy on us.

PRAYER

Hear these petitions, O merciful Jesus, and grant me the grace
to ponder them in my heart, repeat them frequently and learn
from them what is asked of me. May I come to know what you
desire and how I may serve you in my suffering sisters and
brothers. And then, Jesus, may I have the courage to act. Our
Father. Hail Mary. Creed.

PART TWO

Prayers in
the Mercy Spirit

As for the sacred vows, Catherine McAuley cherished them with her whole heart; it was her greatest pleasure to make the Renewal of them, and she used to express this sentiment in her previous instructions to the Sisters. "When we first make our vows," she would say, "it is not surprising if we feel anxious, and pronounce them in a timid, faltering voice, being as yet unacquainted with the full extent of His infinite goodness, to whom we engage ourselves forever — but when we renew them, it ought to be with that tone of joy and confidence that the experience of His unceasing mercies must inspire." This feeling was easily discerned in her manner of reading the Act of Renewal, and also in the joyful way she announced the usual Te Deum afterwards. (Bermondsey Annals)

~

LOVING GOD, in the presence of this community of Mercy, we renew the vows we made at our profession in this Institute of the Sisters of Mercy.

We commit ourselves once more to a life of celibate chastity for the sake of your reign. Acknowledging you as our first and all-encompassing love, we give ourselves in that same love to our sisters in community, to those in need, to our family and friends.

We recommit ourselves to a life of evangelical poverty. Trusting in your divine Providence and following Jesus, who became poor for our sake, we strive to live simply and to seek unity of mind and heart in sharing all we have. We value the resources of the earth and desire to use them in harmony and interdependence with all creation.

We recommit ourselves to a life of obedience within this Institute. Uniting ourselves to Christ, whose obedience led to the redemption of the world, we desire to inform our minds, prepare our hearts for dialogue, listen to one another in love, and accept conversion to your will.

We commit ourselves once more to a life of service through the works of mercy. Enriched by your love, healed by your mercy, and taught by your word, we serve the poor, the sick and the ignorant.

Encouraged and sustained by the fidelity of this
community of Mercy, we rejoice in the continued invitation
to seek justice, to be compassionate, and to reflect your
mercy in our world.

TE DEUM

Based on a fifth-century Matins hymn attributed to Nicetas of Remesiana

~

WE PRAISE you, God. We celebrate your Holy Presence!
All creation bows down in worship before you.
Angels sing your praise. Hosts of heaven, angelic choirs,
    all cherubim and seraphim praise you in unending song.
Holy, holy, holy is God.
All the heavens, and all the earth are filled with the wonder and
    majesty of our God!

Your praises are sung by apostles and prophets,
    by all holy disciples, men and women,
By all the blessed who shed their blood for Christ.
To the end of the earth, your holy people proclaim
    their faith in you.

Gracious One, your majesty is boundless.
Your Son Jesus, true God, is to be adored.
Your Spirit, you sent to be our advocate.

O Christ, you alone are the only beloved Son.
You became flesh to save us. You made your home within
    the virgin's womb.

Destroying death's sting, you opened up heaven to all believers.
You sit at God's right hand in glory. We believe that you will
    come to judge the earth with justice and mercy.

We, therefore, ask your grace and aid, for you shed your blood
for our redemption.
Welcome your servants into the company of saints in glory.

Save your people, God.
Bless those who belong to you.
Be their shepherd. Uphold them and lift them up.
Day by day we praise you. Daily we acclaim you with joy.
We will confess and glorify your holy name now and forever.

In your great mercy, God, throughout this day,
protect us and liberate us from sin's grasp.
Have mercy on us, we pray, have mercy on us!
May your mercy and loving kindness always remain with us.
We have placed our confidence in you. In you alone have
we hoped.
May we not be disappointed. Amen.

NOVENA FOR THE FEAST OF OUR LADY OF MERCY (SEPTEMBER 24)

GOD OF mercy, lover of those who are poor, pour out your
Spirit upon all creation. You sent Jesus to us that we might
know the depths of your love and mercy for us. May we who
have received mercy be mercy for others.

Animated by Catherine McAuley's passion to serve your
suffering people, we have committed ourselves to follow
her example. For the sake of your reign, we have embraced
the Mercy way of life.

As we prepare to celebrate the feast of Mary, the Mother
of Mercy, we ask that you continue to give us hands to heal
and soothe, and ears to hear the longing and anguish of those
who cry out for your justice. Let our hearts be filled with
compassion for the stranger and the outcast. May we be sisters
to one another and to all your sons and daughters.

May what we profess with our lips be proclaimed in
our lives. We ask this in the name of Jesus and through the
intercession of Mary, our Mother of Mercy. Amen.

PRAYER FOR THE INSTITUTE
OF THE SISTERS OF MERCY

O GOD, through the power of your Spirit and under the protection of Mary, Mother of Mercy, you gave the Institute of
Mercy to the church for the relief of persons who are poor, sick,
and ignorant. We ask you to strengthen and enlighten all those
whom you have called to this path of Mercy. May we be faithful
witnesses and sacraments of your love. Through our service
of your people may we grow in mercy and compassion, and
may we enjoy the gift of your holy presence forever. Amen.

LITANY OF PATRON SAINTS

*The patron saints of the Sisters of Mercy are all the holy women and men who
have guided, inspired, helped and prayed for the Sisters of Mercy since our
founding in 1831. Representative of this vast and beloved company are the saints
whom Catherine McAuley and the first Sisters of Mercy named in the original*
Rule and Constitutions of the Institute of Mercy — *as "bright examples" of the
mercifulness to which we are called and as saints of God to whom we have
"particular devotion" (Rule 3.2 and 16.3). The continued intercession of these
saints is sought in the following litany.*

~

GOD OF mercy, God of the poor and suffering, we come to
you in our need. Help us to learn the way of mercy from the
example of the patron saints of our Institute — all those holy
women and men who lived merciful lives in their own times
and places. Form in us, as you once formed in them, the mind
and heart of Christ Jesus.

Jesus, lover of the poor,	have mercy on us
Jesus, healer of the sick,	have mercy on us
Jesus, comforter of the sorrowing,	have mercy on us
Mary, mother of mercy,	pray for us
Mary, blessed among women,	pray for us
Mary, faithful disciple,	pray for us
Saint Joseph,	intercede for us
Saint Ann,	intercede for us
Saint Joachim,	intercede for us
Saint Peter,	intercede for us
Saint Paul,	intercede for us
Saint John the Evangelist,	intercede for us
Saint Patrick,	intercede for us
Saint Bridget of Kildare,	intercede for us
Saint Augustine,	intercede for us
Saint Monica,	intercede for us
Saint Francis de Sales,	intercede for us
Saint Peter Nolasco,	intercede for us
Saint Vincent de Paul,	intercede for us
Saint John of God,	intercede for us
Saint Camillus de Lellis,	intercede for us
Saint Catherine of Genoa,	intercede for us
Saint Joseph Calasanctius,	intercede for us
Saint Angela Merici,	intercede for us
Saint Ignatius Loyola,	intercede for us
Saint Francis Xavier,	intercede for us
Saint Catherine of Siena,	intercede for us
Saint Aloysius Gonzaga,	intercede for us
Venerable Catherine McAuley,	intercede for us
All you holy women of Mercy,	intercede for us

Let us pray:

Gracious God, fill us with the same spirit of compassion and justice that impelled these holy men and women of faith to follow Jesus in the way of love. Have mercy upon your people. Form in us the mind and heart of Christ Jesus. Amen.

PRAYER FOR BENEFACTORS

"If any person . . . does a favor to the Sisters of Mercy or even speaks kindly of their Institute, it must be noted in the Annals and all future generations of the Order must testify gratitude by their prayers for the Benefactor." This comment, taken from Teresa Austin Carroll's Life of Catherine McAuley, *pp. 364–5, is inscribed in the Book of Benefactors, Callaghan Room, Mercy International Centre.*

~

PROVIDENT GOD, pour out your blessings on our benefactors. Their goodness has encouraged us; their gifts have enhanced our efforts to recreate your merciful presence in our world. In gratitude, we ask you to reward them with signs of your generous love and, when their lives on earth are over, to welcome them to your heavenly banquet. Amen.

PRAYER FOR UNION AND CHARITY

GRANT US peace and harmony, O God, and assist us always to preserve union and charity in the midst of our diversity, differences, and difficulties. May the sun never set on our anger; rather, may a spirit of reconciliation dwell among us. Through our experience of your forgiving love may we have the grace both to forgive those who have hurt us and to seek pardon from those whom we have offended. Be with us as we come and go, so that our hearts may always be centered in you. We ask this through Jesus, the gracious sign of your love and forgiveness. Amen.

PRAYER FOR PROTECTION

MARY, MOTHER of Mercy, we pray for safety in our home. May its roof and walls shield us from harm and danger of any kind. May they preserve us from fire and flood and from storms within and without. May its windows reflect the beauty of the world in which you have placed us. May its doors always open wide in hospitality. You created the home in which Jesus grew in wisdom, age and grace. Bless us as we strive to make his life the pattern for our own. We ask this through your loving intercession. Amen.

PRAYER FOR THE CANONIZATION OF CATHERINE McAULEY

LOVING GOD, you chose Catherine McAuley for the service of your people who are poor, sick, and uneducated. You inspired her to found the Institute of Mercy so that these good works might endure. Give to each of us, her daughters, a portion of her compassionate spirit and an ardent desire to serve your suffering people. Bless all our undertakings and grant that union and charity may always thrive among us. Graciously hear our prayer for Catherine, and by granting the favors we ask through her intercession, hasten the day when her sanctity will be celebrated by all the church. Amen.

PRAYER FOR RELIGIOUS VOCATIONS

GOD OF mercy, you have called us to fullness of life through Christ Jesus. Deep within us you speak the word that invites us to continue the mission of Jesus, to make your love known throughout the world. Send your Spirit, loving God, to stir up our courage to carry on that mission.

God of the harvest, raise up within the church women and men who will commit their lives to serving your people. Send to our Mercy Institute women of fidelity and compassion who will join us in our vowed commitment to serve the poor, sick, and ignorant. Bless us also with associates who will share our Mercy mission. May we rejoice in their call and support them through the witness of our lives and the hospitality of our hearts.

Remember the works of our deceased sisters and their trust in your providence. Through their intercession send us new members to continue what you began through Catherine McAuley. This we ask in the name of Jesus and for the sake of your people. Amen.

PRAYER FOR A SISTER PREPARING FOR PROFESSION OF VOWS

GOD OF mercy, you have called (N._____) to accept your invitation to follow you in lifelong consecration as a Sister of Mercy. Be with her now as she prepares to make her commitment to serve the poor, sick and ignorant. Send her the spirit of wisdom to help her know your desire for her. Send her the spirit of generosity to say "yes" as Mary did. Send her the spirit of courage to choose what is still unfolding. As she prepares to profess her vows, may she find encouragement and support in our shared Mercy life. May we, her sisters, be reanimated by her example to deepen our own commitment and renew our desire to live our lives centered in you. Amen.

PRAYER FOR SISTERS IN LEADERSHIP

HOLY WISDOM, Spirit of truth, be with our sisters who have been called to the ministry of leadership. Strengthen them to do what is needed to further the reign of justice and mercy in our world. Give them words that animate and challenge us to action. Give them vision and perception to read the signs of our times. Give them hearts of compassion to understand the needs of your suffering people.

God of mercy, stir up in them the same passion that impelled Catherine McAuley to respond to the needs of her time. May her spirit find expression in them. Protect them from weariness and discouragement. Bless them with the sure knowledge of your presence and providence, now and always. This we ask in the name of Jesus. Amen.

PRAYER FOR NEW MINISTRIES

LOVING GOD, you have promised to be with us as we journey. You helped those who have gone before us to establish ministries that served your people. In times of hardship, scarcity and joy, you were with them and blessed their efforts. We ask your blessing upon this new ministry so that what you now begin in us may prosper through your life-giving Spirit. May we always desire what you will. If it pleases you, may this ministry flourish and bring life to your people. This we ask of you, confident that whatever we ask in the name of Jesus will be granted. Amen.

PRAYER FOR GUIDANCE

COME, O life-giving Spirit, transform us. Stir up in us the flame of love which is your gift. Give us wisdom to see as you see. Give us understanding to hear as you hear. Give us courage and strength to walk the way of justice and integrity. Kindle in us wonder and awe, that we may have grateful spirits. You who dwell within us, praying unceasingly, fill us with love and devotion. Holy Wisdom, guide us in the choices we must make. Give us discerning hearts that we may choose what is good, in accord with your desire. Loving God of mercy, finish in us the work you have begun. Amen.

The Sisters of Mercy throughout the world owe a great debt of gratitude to the
women who founded the first Convent of Mercy on Baggot Street, Dublin, and
the nine additional foundations established during the lifetime of Catherine
McAuley. From these ten houses subsequently came all the future communities
of Mercy. Inspired by the courage, mercifulness and self-sacrifice of these first
Mercy Founders and of their descendants, we pray for the continuation of their
brave spirit of founding in our own lives.

~

WOMEN OF mercy throughout all time,
  we, your sisters, ask you to draw near to us in these days.
May the legacy of your love and commitment be our treasure.
May your passion for the poor be our passion.
May your lives poured out in the service of your brothers and
  sisters be a light and witness to us.

Spirit of Mercy,	live in us
Spirit of Catherine,	animate us
Mothers of Mercy,	pray for us
Catherine McAuley,	pray for us
Mary Ann Doyle,	pray for us
Mary Elizabeth Harley,	pray for us
Mary Angela Dunne,	pray for us
Mary Frances Warde,	pray for us
Mary Clare Moore,	pray for us
Mary Elizabeth Moore,	pray for us
Mary Teresa White,	pray for us
Mary Aloysius Scott,	pray for us
Mary Juliana Hardman,	pray for us

Add the names of the holy women who have established
your communities.

PRAYER

God of mercy, you have given us the gift of the memory and
deeds of these faithful women. Through the example of their

loving kindness and compassion may we be inspired to center our lives in you and to extend your merciful love to your people. May those who have taught us how to live mercy strengthen us through their intercession. This we ask in the name of Jesus. Amen.

LITANY OF THE BLESSED VIRGIN MARY

LORD, HAVE mercy on us. Christ, have mercy on us.
Christ, hear us. Christ, graciously hear us.
God, the Father of heaven, have mercy on us.
God the Son, Redeemer of the world, have mercy on us.
God the Holy Spirit, have mercy on us.
Holy Trinity, one God, have mercy on us.

Holy Mary,	pray for us
Holy Mother of God,	pray for us
Holy Virgin of virgins,	pray for us
Mother of Christ,	pray for us
Mother of divine grace,	pray for us
Mother most pure,	pray for us
Mother most chaste,	pray for us
Mother inviolate,	pray for us
Mother undefiled,	pray for us
Mother most amiable,	pray for us
Mother most admirable,	pray for us
Mother of mercy,	pray for us
Mother of good counsel,	pray for us
Mother of our Creator,	pray for us
Mother of our Redeemer,	pray for us
Virgin most prudent,	pray for us
Virgin most venerable,	pray for us
Virgin most renowned,	pray for us
Virgin most powerful,	pray for us
Virgin most merciful,	pray for us

Virgin most faithful,	pray for us
Mirror of justice,	pray for us
Seat of wisdom,	pray for us
Cause of our joy,	pray for us
Spiritual vessel,	pray for us
Vessel of honor,	pray for us
Vessel of singular devotion,	pray for us
Mystical rose,	pray for us
Tower of David,	pray for us
Tower of ivory,	pray for us
House of gold,	pray for us
Ark of the covenant,	pray for us
Gate of heaven,	pray for us
Morning star,	pray for us
Health of the sick,	pray for us
Refuge of sinners,	pray for us
Comforter of the afflicted,	pray for us
Help of Christians,	pray for us
Queen of angels,	pray for us
Queen of patriarchs,	pray for us
Queen of prophets,	pray for us
Queen of apostles,	pray for us
Queen of martyrs,	pray for us
Queen of confessors,	pray for us
Queen of virgins,	pray for us
Queen of all saints,	pray for us
Queen conceived without original sin,	pray for us
Queen assumed into heaven,	pray for us
Queen of the most holy rosary,	pray for us
Queen of peace,	pray for us

Lamb of God, who take away the sins of the world,
    spare us, O Lord.
Lamb of God, who take away the sins of the world,
    graciously hear us, O Lord.

Lamb of God, who take away the sins of the world,
   have mercy on us.

LEADER: Pray for us, O holy Mother of God.
ALL: That we may be made worthy of the promises
              of Christ.

Let us pray:

O God, we beseech you, grant that we, your servants, may enjoy health of mind and body; and by the intercession of blessed Mary, ever virgin, may we come to the enjoyment of everlasting gladness. Through Christ our Lord. Amen.

PART THREE

Rituals Marking
the Death of a Sister

LEADER: I know that my Redeemer lives and on the last day
I shall rise again.

ALL: In my body I shall look on God, my Savior.

LEADER: We shall look upon our God,

ALL: And savor the sweetness of eternal life.

LEADER: Glory to you, God of the dead and of the living.
Glory to you, Jesus, the first-born of creation.
Glory to you, indwelling Spirit, who make your
home in us.

ALL: As it was in the beginning, is now and will be forever.
Amen.

LEADER: Long ago (N. ____) was welcomed into this community of Mercy. She journeyed with us as we sought
to serve God through doing the works of compassion,
helping to free those in bondage, teaching, preaching
and healing in God's name.

At her baptism, (N. ____) received life in Christ
Jesus. May this candle, a symbol of the Risen Lord,
remind us of Christ's presence in her life and of
the light she was to us and to all the world.

(lighting of the candle)

Through the waters of baptism she was welcomed
into the community of faith. With this holy water
we bless her again, trusting that the ever-flowing water
of eternal life now carries her into the arms of her
Creator.

(sprinkling of the body)

(N. ____) entrusted all to God and offered her
life in the mission of mercy by her vows of poverty,
consecrated chastity, obedience, and service. We
place in her hands the testament of her dedication,
which she signed on the day of her profession.
May she enjoy the rewards of a life lived with fidelity.

(placement of her vows)

(N. ____) shared in the death and rising of Christ
Jesus. As God bestowed mercy upon her, so she
radiated mercy to God's people. As we place upon
her the Mercy Cross, let us pray that she may join
the company of our sisters in whose footsteps
she followed.

(placement of the Mercy Cross)

SCRIPTURE READING

Matthew 11:28–30
John 14:1–3
Romans 6:8–9
or any other selection

LEADER: May God's mercy surround us with peace.
ALL: May God comfort us in our loss.

LEADER: Let us pray:
ALL: God of mercy, you are the loving God who gave
(N. ____) life by breathing into her your own divine
breath. She served you faithfully all her days, and
now you have called her home to rest in you. We ask
that in your compassion you keep vigil with us as we
mourn this sister whom we have greatly loved. May
this time of grieving be tempered by our joy in having
known and loved her. May our memories of her
strengthen us as we return her to you, our loving God.

LEADER: May the love of God and the peace of Christ Jesus
bless and console us and wipe every tear from our
eyes. We ask this in the name of the Father and
of the Son and of the Holy Spirit.

ALL: Amen.

A closing song is recommended.

RITUAL FOR A TIME OF REMEMBRANCE

GATHERING SONG

A theme of remembrance or thanksgiving.

LEADER: We join together at this moment to honor the life
of our Sister (N. _____). We praise her faith, her hope,
her love of God and her devotion to God's people.
(N. ____) was a daughter of Catherine McAuley and
shared Catherine's commitment to the poor, suffering,
and uneducated. As we gather to remember the
goodness of her life, let us recall that we are not alone.
We come together with all our Sisters who have
gone before us and now join us in celebrating this
sacred passage.

READING I

*Select one of the following readings from the letters of Catherine
McAuley to Sister Mary Elizabeth Moore about the death
of Sister Mary Teresa Potter in Limerick on March 20, 1840. In
reading C, Catherine recalls the death of Sister Mary Frances
Marmion on March 10, 1840.*

A. My darling Sister M. Elizabeth,
I did not think any event in this world could make me
feel so much. I have cried heartily and implored God to
comfort you. I know He will. This has not been done

in anger. Some joyful circumstance will soon prove that God is watching over your concerns, which are all his own, but without the Cross the real Crown cannot come. Some great thing which [God] designs to accomplish would have been too much without a little bitter in the cup. Bless and love the Fatherly hand which has hurt you. He will soon come with both hands filled with favors and blessings. *(Neumann, ed. 204)*

B. Your last letter was a great comfort to me. When I read it in the community room all exclaimed: "I don't know who would not like to die under such circumstances. Oh, that is not death." They were astonished and delighted. [The funeral] was indeed a heavenly ceremony, more so than any Reception or Profession. It was like a grand entrance into Paradise. Thanks be to God you had such solid consolation. It will be a powerful attraction to many to put themselves in the way of such a blessed departure from this passing world. I have never heard of anything like it. *(Neumann, ed. 205)*

C. Mr. Mulhall . . . came to see us on the death of our dear Sister M. F. [Sr. M. Frances Marmion] and said: "I congratulate you. You have or will soon have another friend in heaven. How delightful to be forming a community there!" I asked him would it be wrong to hope that it was now formed. He answered: "What are they here for but to prepare for heaven. They ought to go as soon as they are ready, to make room for poor souls that are in the midst of danger. There is no other way of carrying on this holy traffic so as to meet the designs of God. It is [God's] own Divine plan." *(Neumann, ed. 205)*

Here is a call for the endurance of the saints, those who keep the commandments of God and hold fast to the faith of Jesus. And I heard a voice from heaven saying, "Write this: Blessed are the dead who die in the Lord." "Yes," says the Spirit, "they will rest from their labors, for their deeds follow them."

LEADER: Our Sister (N. _____) held fast to the faith of Jesus and is now at rest in the Lord. Let us now honor her memory and encourage one another with stories of her deeds of mercy and fidelity.

At the end of the sharing, all pray:

ALL: God of mercy, fill us with thankfulness for the gift of (N. _____) to us, and for all that she has been to us. We come to this moment with sadness and joy. While we feel the sorrow of this loss, we rejoice that her life is not ended but transformed. With hearts full of trust we hold out our hands to the mystery of death and resurrection. Jesus, our life and hope, receive our grief as your own, you who knew the death of friends and the promises of God.

We thank you for this woman who trusted that you would be with her, in life and in death. We praise you, O God, who, in your tender love, asked her to return home to you.

May she join all our sisters who have gone before us. They have marked out for us the path of mercy. May they now show us how to embrace this passing. This we ask in faith, we who are yours for time and eternity. Amen.

LEADER: Blessed be our God who saves.
Blessed be the God of everlasting life.

ALL: Blessed be the waters that brought us to birth
in Christ Jesus.
Blessed be the light that guided us on our way.
Blessed be all those who witnessed to us their trust
in God.

LEADER: We bring the body of our sister (N. ____) to this
hallowed place. We return it to the earth from which
it was shaped by our loving Creator, who gave it
form and beauty. We lay her body in this holy ground,
and with reverence we bless her.

*The reverencing of the body is done by an appropriate ritual,
such as sprinkling water, placing flowers, or sprinkling earth on
the casket.*

READING: JOHN 17:24

Father, I desire that those also, whom you have given me, may
be with me where I am, to see my glory, which you have given
me because you loved me before the foundation of the world.

LEADER: All praise to you, God of all creation.
Praise to you, holy and living God.
We praise and bless you for your mercy
and loving kindness.
Holy are you.

ALL: Blessed be our God who saves.

LEADER: You open to us the gates of righteousness
and lead us to the dwellings of the saints.
You make a home for those who love you.
Holy and blessed are you.

ALL: Blessed be our God who saves.

LEADER: We praise you, our refuge and strength.
We bless you, our God and Redeemer.
Your praise is always in our hearts and on our lips.
You are our hope. Holy are you and blessed.

ALL: Blessed be our God who saves.

LEADER: As we leave this holy place we carry with us the living memory of (N. _____) and of all those holy women who have gone before us and who now live a new and glorious life. We commend their spirits to God and to all who have loved them and now remember them.

LITANY OF HOLY WOMEN

Mary of Nazareth, pray for us
Mary Magdalen, pray for us
Mary and Martha of Bethany, pray for us
Catherine McAuley, pray for us

Add the names of sisters who have recently died, ending with the name of the one being buried.

LEADER: Loving and merciful God, hear the prayers for our sister (N. _____). By her faith and hope she has always been united with you, her Creator. By her generous service she has been a loving disciple of Jesus Christ. By her strong and enabling love she has witnessed to your holy Spirit. Receive her now into the fullness of your presence. Give comfort to all of us who mourn her passing from our midst, for we believe that you will raise us all on the last day. And so with Jesus we pray: Our Father . . .

LEADER: May God grant (N. _____) eternal life and joy.

ALL: May the mercy of God enfold her, and the love
of God surround her. May she be our companion
on our way, until we meet face to face in God.

A final hymn, such as the Salve Regina or Suscipe, is sung.

Salve, Regina, mater misericordiae;
    vita, dulcedo, et spes nostra, salve,
Ad te clamamus, exsules filii Hevae.
Ad te suspiramus, gementes et flentes
    in hac lacrimarum valle.
Eia ergo, Advocata nostra,
    illos tuos misericordes oculos
    ad nos converte.
Et Jesum, benedictum fructum ventris tui,
    nobis post hoc exsilium ostende.
O clemens, O pia, O dulcis Virgo Maria.

PART FOUR

The Prayers of
Catherine McAuley

The prayers of Catherine McAuley (1778 – 1841) are of
two kinds: particular prayers, found in the printed prayerbooks
of her day, that she is known to have prayed often and that
were said to be among her "favorite" prayers; and the prayers
that she herself composed, either completely or in part.

The *Practical Sayings, Advices and Prayers of our Revered
Foundress, Mother Mary Catharine* [sic] *McAuley* was compiled
and published in 1868 by one of Catherine McAuley's earliest
associates, Mary Clare Moore, the superior of the Convent
of Mercy that Catherine had founded in Bermondsey, London,
in 1839. Clare had become affiliated with Catherine at the
House of Mercy on Baggot Street, Dublin, in 1828; after a year's
absence she joined the resident community in June 1830. While
Catherine, Mary Ann Doyle and Elizabeth Harley made their
novitiate at the Presentation Convent on George's Hill, Dublin
(September 1830 to December 1831), prior to founding the
Sisters of Mercy on December 12, 1831, Clare remained at Baggot
Street. She was, therefore, one of the first group of women,
seven in number, who were received into the Sisters of Mercy in
the ceremony held at Baggot Street on January 23, 1832. Clare

lived with Catherine at Baggot Street for the next five years, until she became the first superior of the Mercy community founded in Cork in 1837. She remained in Cork for two years and then went with Catherine to found the community in Bermondsey. Except for two brief periods, she was the superior of the Bermondsey community until her death in 1874.

Thus Clare knew Catherine well. She knew her habits of personal prayer, and she knew the communal prayers Catherine had chosen for the first Sisters of Mercy. In the *Practical Sayings* she records some of the prayers Catherine composed (pp. 32 – 34). While she does not present Catherine's "Act of Consecration," she notes that "For her private devotions she had only *The Devotions to the Sacred Heart* (the edition translated by Rev. Joseph Joy Dean), which she used for Mass, preparation for Holy Communion, etc." (p. 35). When Catherine acquired her copy of the Joseph Joy Dean, SJ, edition of *Devotions to the Sacred Heart of Jesus* (Dublin: Chambers and Hallagan, 1820) is not precisely known; however, in a letter written on September 1, 1844, Clare Moore refers to this book when she describes the morning prayer of the Baggot Street community after the dedication of the Chapel on June 4, 1829: "At six we assembled in choir and said morning prayer, which was only the Act of Oblation from the big *Sacred Heart* book." It is this "Act of Oblation" that Catherine McAuley transcribed in her own hand, with many alterations, as "An Act of Consecration." Catherine's own copy of *Devotions to the Sacred Heart of Jesus* is now preserved in the Archives of the Sisters of Mercy in Limerick. On the printed text of the "Act of Oblation," she has written some of the many revisions that appear in her manuscript of "An Act of Consecration." The manuscript itself is in the Archives of the Sisters of Mercy of the Americas, in Silver Spring, Maryland.

In the *Practical Sayings,* Clare Moore also notes that Catherine McAuley's "Favourite Prayers" were:
The Thirty Days' Prayer in honour of our
    divine Lord, and that also in honour of our Blessed Lady

The Psalter of Jesus
The Universal Prayer
The Seven Penitential Psalms, with the Paraphrase
    by Fr. [Francis] Blyth (p. 34)

We know from the memoirs of the earliest Sisters of Mercy, including Clare Moore's, that among printed prayers, "The Psalter of Jesus" was Catherine's "favourite" prayer as early as her years at Coolock, long before she founded the House of Mercy on Baggot Street, and that it remained so during the early years of the House of Mercy and during the decade of the 1830s, after she founded the Sisters of Mercy. When she first came to use the two "Thirty Days' Prayers" — to the Redeemer, and to the Blessed Virgin Mary — or the "Universal Prayer for All Things Necessary to Salvation" is not exactly known. However, the "Psalter of Jesus," the "Universal Prayer" and the "Thirty Days' Prayer to the Blessed Virgin Mary" are all contained in William Gahan's *The Christian's Guide to Heaven; or A Complete Manual of Catholic Piety* (Dublin: T. M'Donnel, 1804). Clare Moore refers to this prayerbook in her August 23, 1844 letter, when she describes the prayer of the Baggot Street community in 1828–29: "We said every morning the prayers in Gahan's *Catholic Piety,* made meditation; at night, prayers out of the same, and a lecture by Revd. Mother, who always said the prayers and read." It is clear, from Catherine's own letters as well as Clare Moore's, that Catherine prayed the two Thirty Days' Prayers every day for a month, with the respective communities, at the founding of each new convent of Sisters of Mercy. The "Universal Prayer for All Things Necessary to Salvation," composed by Pope Clement XI (1700–1721), is included in most nineteenth-century versions of the *Choir Manual of the Sisters of Mercy* and is presumably a community prayer chosen from the beginning by Catherine McAuley. All of these prayers which were so meaningful to her are contained in the standard Catholic prayerbooks available in Ireland in the early nineteenth century.

Clare Moore also lists among Catherine's favorite prayers "The Seven Penitential Psalms, with the Paraphrase by Fr. [Francis] Blyth." In the Vulgate numbering, as Catherine would have known them, the seven penitential psalms are Psalms 6, 31 (NRSV 32), 37 (NRSV 38), 50 (NRSV 51), 101 (NRSV 102), 129 (NRSV 130) and 142 (NRSV 143). The long tradition of praying Psalm 129 (NRSV 130) daily in all communities of Sisters of Mercy — "Out of the depths I have cried to you, O Lord; Lord, hear my voice" — undoubtedly evolved from Catherine's devotion to these seven psalms; and the numerous references in these psalms to human afflictions and to God's plenteous mercy served to ground the charism of the first Sisters of Mercy in its biblical expressions. The seventh edition of Francis Blyth's *A Devout Paraphrase of the Seven Penitential Psalms; or, A Practical Guide to Repentance* was published in Dublin by the Catholic Book Society in 1835. Catherine McAuley had presumably obtained an earlier edition of his book, perhaps from one of her Carmelite friends at St. Teresa Church, Clarendon Street, Dublin. Blyth (1705? – 1772) was a Discalced Carmelite.

In the pages that follow, the prayers of Catherine McAuley — both those she composed and those she frequently prayed — are offered for the use of those who wish to pray with her, in the language she used and in her spirit. The prayers she herself composed are given exactly as she wrote them; the prayers that she found in the prayerbooks of her day, as noted after each prayer, are given exactly as they appear in the particular prayerbooks she used or may have used. Those who wish to include these prayers in their own personal or communal prayer are invited to adapt them slightly to reflect present-day Christian vocabulary and theological emphases.

MORNING OFFERING

O MY most compassionate Lord and Saviour Jesus Christ,
I humbly beseech thee to look on me this day with pity, and
grant me the grace to be pleasing and acceptable to thee even
for one moment.

PRAYER FOR A SISTER
DANGEROUSLY ILL

MY GOD, look down with mercy and pity on our dear Sister
afflicted with sickness. Give her perfect resignation to thy divine
Will, and graciously enable her to suffer without complaining
whatever thou art pleased to appoint. Compassionate Lord Jesus,
support and comfort her.

Blessed Mother of God and all ye happy saints, intercede
for her, that she may pass through this time of trial so as to
purify her heart from the smallest stain, that at the hour of her
departure from this miserable world she may enter on the joys
of a happy eternity. Amen.

FOR A SISTER IN RETREAT, BEFORE
RECEPTION OR PROFESSION

ALMIGHTY AND most merciful God, we earnestly beg thy grace
and blessing for our Sister in Retreat. Assist her, we humbly
beseech thee, to accomplish thy holy Will; direct her particularly
in what she is about to undertake, and teach her to act in the
manner most pleasing to thy Divine Majesty. Enlighten her by
thy wisdom, support her by thy power, and by thine infinite
goodness direct all her exertions on this occasion to thy greater
glory and her own eternal salvation. Amen.

A FAVORITE ASPIRATION

MORTIFY IN me, dear Jesus, all that displeases thee, and make me according to thine own heart's desire.

~

The above prayers are presented in A Little Book of the Practical Sayings, Advices and Prayers of our Revered Foundress, Mother Mary Catharine [sic] McAuley, *compiled and published by Mary Clare Moore (London: Burns, Oates & Co., 1868).*

A PRAYER FOR POOR PEOPLE

MY GOD, look down with pity and mercy on your afflicted poor, and grant us grace to do all that we can for their relief and comfort. We most humbly ask your blessing this day — in the name and for the sake of our Lord and Saviour Jesus Christ. Amen.

~

This prayer was composed by Catherine McAuley about 1838. The card on which Catherine wrote the prayer is in the Archives of the Sisters of Mercy, Burlingame, California.

PRAYER BEFORE MEDITATION

COME HOLY Ghost, take possession of our hearts and kindle in them the fire of thy divine love. Oh Eternal Father, shed upon us, we beseech thee, the plenitude of thy divine Spirit, and give us an entire and perfect submission to the inspiration of thy Grace. We renounce from the bottom of our hearts every thought and affection that may withdraw us from thy adorable presence, and we most earnestly implore, through the merits and sufferings of our Lord Jesus Christ, and the intercession of His sacred and immaculate Mother, our Angel Guardians and

Patron Saints, that this meditation may conduce to thy glory and our eternal salvation.

~

Catherine McAuley wrote this prayer on a blank page in the front of her copy of A Journal of Meditations for Every Day in the Year, Gathered out of Divers Authors *(London, 1630; and Dublin: Richard Coyne, 1823). Catherine's book is now preserved in the Archives of the Sisters of Mercy, Tullamore, with the following notation by one of the early sisters in the Tullamore community: "This Meditation Book belonged to our Venerated Foundress, who left it after her in one of her visits to Tullamore, about the year 1839 or 1840. It has ever been regarded as a precious remembrance of such a holy Religious and is particularly dear to us, her unworthy children."*

Catherine's Journal of Meditations *was used as the morning meditation book of the Baggot Street community after Catherine moved there, especially after the dedication of the chapel in June 1829. As Clare Moore notes in her letter of September 1, 1844: "At six we assembled in choir and said morning prayer, which was only the Act of Oblation . . . then Meditation in the* Journal *'till 7 I think." In the Derry Large Manuscript, Mary Ann Doyle also says that their morning prayer "consisted chiefly of the Act of Oblation . . . followed by a meditation from the* Journal." *The texts of the meditations in the* Journal *are biblically oriented. Before Catherine read the daily text to the community, she evidently prayed on their behalf this preparatory "Prayer before Meditation."*

THE SUSCIPE OR ACT OF RESIGNATION

MY GOD, I am thine for all eternity. Teach me to cast my whole self into the arms of thy Providence with the most lively, unlimited confidence in thy compassionate, tender pity. Grant, O most Merciful Redeemer, that whatever thou dost ordain or permit may always be acceptable to me. Take from my heart all painful anxiety; suffer nothing to afflict me, but sin; nothing to delight me, but the hope of coming to the possession of thee, my God, in thy own everlasting kingdom. Amen.

~

This text of Catherine McAuley's prayer is found in the Limerick Manuscript written by Mary Vincent Harnett. This prayer is also found in the Practical Sayings, Advices and Prayers of . . . Catharine [sic] McAuley, *compiled by Mary Clare Moore (London: Burns, Oates & Co., 1868). In the* Practical

Sayings, *where the prayer is titled "Act of Resignation," the word "unbounded"*
is used where "unlimited" appears here, and there is one other very minor
difference in wording. Although her attitudes are faithfully preserved in musical
versions of this prayer, Catherine's exact wording is adapted (see Sullivan,
Catherine McAuley and the Tradition of Mercy, *389, n. 7).*

AN ACT OF CONSECRATION

OH THOU God of my heart, my whole desire and only portion
consist in loving thee. To thee I now devote myself — without
any reserve and forever.

I consecrate to thee my heart — receive it as an acceptable
sacrifice. I conjure thee to preserve and unite it to thine, for
with thee I desire to reside all the days of my life — to live in
future unknown to the world and known only to thee.

To thee I consecrate my will, that it may be conformable to
thine in all things — what should I desire or will but the will of
my Lord and God. Oh dear Jesus, may thy will be done. Let
self will reign no longer in me. Thou art my Lord, my Saviour,
my Father — I wish henceforth to be thy grateful obedient
child. Behold me now entirely at thy disposal.

I consecrate to thee my understanding. I shall no longer
judge of any thing but according to thy divine lights. I shall
despise all thou hast despised, and esteem what thou hast
esteemed. I shall feel only contempt for the false treasures, the
vain honors and fatal pleasures of this world. I shall desire only
the good things of Heaven, and the means which conduct to
them — disengagement from creatures, humiliations and crosses.
Such are now the objects of my ambition — oh my God, may
thy grace work in me the accomplishment of the holy desires
with which it inspires me.

I consecrate my memory to thee. It shall always remind
me of thine infinite perfections — thy goodness — thy supreme
attractions. I shall place my delight in the remembrance of
thy favors — of thy love and thy mercy to me — could I use any

means more effectual to penetrate me with love and gratitude towards thee.

I consecrate to thee my body. Purify it more and more, and render it worthy of being the Temple of the Holy Ghost. Oh Jesus, I now surrender it to thee — dispose of it according to thy Blessed Will. I submit freely to all mortifications — infirmities — sickness — sorrows — and death. I desire nothing but what thou desirest — and however painful the cross may be which thou hast prepared for me, I await it through thy grace with entire submission. I shall receive it with lively gratitude — carry it with joy and constancy, happy in being able to say, with the great Apostle — "with Christ I am nailed to the Cross."

I consecrate to thee, sweet Jesus, all that I might ever possess in earthly goods — authority or influence — all is thine — dispose of me as thou pleasest. I consecrate to thee all that I can — joys — sorrows — life and death — to testify to thee my love, and far as I am able to induce all hearts to love thee. Mercifully vouchsafe to receive me. I am now resolved — with the help of thy grace, oh my God — to be thine without any reserve or division and to serve thee with lively devotion to the last hour of my existence. Amen.

~

This is Catherine McAuley's own handwritten and revised transcription of "An Act of Oblation" contained in her own prayerbook: Joseph Joy Dean, SJ, ed., Devotions to the Sacred Heart of Jesus *(Dublin: Chambers and Hallagan, 1820), pp. 267 – 70. The Baggot Street community prayed this Act together every morning, from at least as early as 1829. For an account of the revisions Catherine made in the text as it appears in Dean's* Devotions, *see "Catherine McAuley's Spiritual Reading and Prayers,"* Irish Theological Quarterly *57.2 (1991): 124 – 46.*

This prayer is printed in Mary Ignatia Neumann, RSM, ed., Letters of Catherine McAuley *(Baltimore: Helicon Press, 1969), pp. 392 – 93, and in Mary Angela Bolster, RSM, ed.,* The Correspondence of Catherine McAuley *(Cork: The Sisters of Mercy of the Dioceses of Cork and Ross, 1989), pp. 7 – 8. The text given above is that of Catherine McAuley's own manuscript, which is in the Archives of the Sisters of Mercy of the Americas, Silver Springs, Maryland. The wording of this text is slightly different from the previously printed texts.*

THE PSALTER OF JESUS

FIRST PART

"At the name of Jesus let every knee bend, both in heaven, on earth, and under the earth; and let every tongue acknowledge that the Lord Jesus Christ is in the glory of God the Father."
Philippians 2:10 – 11

THE FIRST PETITION

Jesus! *(repeated ten times)* thou God of compassion, have mercy on me, and forgive the many and great offences I have committed in thy sight. Many have been the follies of my life, and great are the miseries I have deserved for my ingratitude. Have mercy on me, dear Jesus, for I am weak; heal me, O Lord, for I am unable to help myself. Deliver me from an inordinate affection for any of thy creatures, which may divert mine eyes from incessantly looking up to thee. For the love of thee, grant me henceforth the grace to hate sin; and out of a just esteem of thee, to despise all worldly vanities.

Have mercy on all sinners, I beseech thee, dear Jesus; turn their vices into virtues, and making them sincere lovers of thee, and observers of thy law, conduct them to bliss in everlasting glory. For the sake of thy glorious name, Jesus, and through the merits of thy bitter passion, have mercy also on the souls in purgatory. O Blessed Trinity, one eternal God, have mercy on me. Our Father. Hail, Mary.

THE SECOND PETITION

Jesus! *(repeated ten times)* help me to overcome all temptations to sin, and the malice of my ghostly enemy. Help me to spend my time in virtuous actions, and in such labours as are acceptable to thee. Enable me to resist and repel every inordinate emotion of sloth, gluttony, and carnality. Render my heart enamoured of virtue, and inflamed with desire of thy glorious presence. Help me to merit and preserve a good name by a peaceable and pious life, to thy honour, O Jesus! to my own comfort, and the edification of others.

Have mercy on all sinners, I beseech thee, dear Jesus; turn their vices into virtues, and making them sincere lovers of thee, and observers of thy law, conduct them to bliss in everlasting glory. For the sake of thy glorious name, Jesus, and through the merits of thy bitter passion, have mercy also on the souls in purgatory. O Blessed Trinity, one eternal God, have mercy on me. Our Father. Hail, Mary.

THE THIRD PETITION

Jesus! *(repeated ten times)* grant me effectual strength of soul and body, to please thee in the performance of such virtuous actions as may bring me to thy everlasting joy and felicity. Grant me, O most merciful Saviour, a firm purpose to amend my life, and to make atonement for the years past; those years, alas! which I have lavished, to thy displeasure, in vain or wicked thoughts, evil words, deeds, and habits. Make my heart obedient to thy will, and ready, for thy love, to perform all the works of mercy. Grant me the gifts of the Holy Ghost, which, through a virtuous life, and a devout frequenting of thy most holy sacraments, may at length conduct me to thy heavenly kingdom.

Have mercy on all sinners, I beseech thee, dear Jesus; turn their vices into virtues, and making them sincere lovers of thee, and observers of thy law, conduct them to bliss in everlasting glory. For the sake of thy glorious name, Jesus, and through the merits of thy bitter passion, have mercy also on the souls in purgatory. O Blessed Trinity, one eternal God, have mercy on me. Our Father. Hail, Mary.

THE FOURTH PETITION

Jesus! *(repeated ten times)* comfort me, and grant me grace to fix in thee my chief joy and only felicity; inspire me with heavenly meditations, spiritual sweetness, and fervent desires of thy glory; ravish my soul with the contemplation of heaven, where

I hope to dwell everlastingly with thee. Bring thy unspeakable goodness to my frequent recollection, and let me always with gratitude remember thy gifts; but when thou bringest the multitude of the sins, whereby I have so ungratefully offended thee, to sad remembrance, comfort me with the assurance of pardon, and by the spirit of true penance purging away my guilt, prepare me for the possession of thy heavenly kingdom.

Have mercy on all sinners, I beseech thee, dear Jesus; turn their vices into virtues, and making them sincere lovers of thee, and observers of thy law, conduct them to bliss in everlasting glory. For the sake of thy glorious name, Jesus, and through the merits of thy bitter passion, have mercy also on the souls in purgatory. O Blessed Trinity, one eternal God, have mercy on me. Our Father. Hail, Mary.

THE FIFTH PETITION

Jesus! *(repeated ten times)* make me constant in Faith, Hope, and Charity. Grant me perseverance in virtue, and a resolution never to offend thee. May the memory of thy passion, and of those bitter pains thou didst suffer for my sake, fortify my patience and refresh my soul under every tribulation and adversity. Render me a strenuous professor of the Catholic Faith, and a diligent frequenter of my religious duties. Let me not be blinded by the delights of a deceitful world, nor my fortitude [be] shaken by internal frauds or carnal temptations. My heart has for ever fixed its repose in thee, and resolved to contemn all things for thine eternal rewards.

Have mercy on all sinners, I beseech thee, dear Jesus; turn their vices into virtues, and making them sincere lovers of thee, and observers of thy law, conduct them to bliss in everlasting glory. For the sake of thy glorious name, Jesus, and through the merits of thy bitter passion, have mercy also on the souls in purgatory. O Blessed Trinity, one eternal God, have mercy on me. Our Father.

"The Lord Jesus Christ for our sakes, became obedient unto death, even the death of the cross." *Philippians 2:8*

Hear these petitions, O most merciful Saviour, and grant me the grace frequently to repeat and consider them, that they may serve as so many easy steps, whereby my soul may ascend to thy knowledge and love, and to a diligent performance of my duty to thee and my neighbour, through the whole course of my life. Amen. Our Father. Hail, Mary. I believe in God.

SECOND PART

"At the name of Jesus let every knee bend, both in heaven, on earth, and under the earth; and let every tongue acknowledge that the Lord Jesus Christ is in the glory of God the Father." *Philippians 2:10–11*

THE SIXTH PETITION

Jesus! *(repeated ten times)* enlighten me with spiritual wisdom, whereby I may arrive at a knowledge of thy goodness, and of every thing which is most acceptable to thee. Grant me a perfect apprehension of my only good, and a discretion to regulate my life accordingly. Grant me wisely to proceed from virtue to virtue, till at length I enjoy a clear sight of thy glory. Forbid it, dear Lord, that I return to the sins of which I accused myself at the tribunal of confession. Let others be edified by my pious example, and my enemies mollified by my good counsel.

Have mercy on all sinners, I beseech thee, dear Jesus; turn their vices into virtues, and making them sincere lovers of thee, and observers of thy law, conduct them to bliss in everlasting glory. For the sake of thy glorious name, Jesus, and through the merits of thy bitter passion, have mercy also on the souls in purgatory. O Blessed Trinity, one eternal God, have mercy on me. Our Father. Hail, Mary.

Jesus! *(repeated ten times)* grant me grace inwardly to fear thee, and avoid every occasion whatsoever of offending thee. Let the threats of the torments prepared for sinners, the dread of the loss of thy love and of thy heavenly inheritance, always keep me in awe. Suffer me not to slumber in sin, but rather rouse me to repentance, lest, through thine anger, I may be overtaken by the sentence of eternal wrath, and endless damnation. Let the powerful intercession of thy blessed Mother and of all thy Saints, but above all, thine own merits and mercy, serve as a rampart between my poor soul and thine avenging justice. Enable me, O my God! to work out my salvation with fear and trembling, and let the apprehension of thy sacred judgments make me a more humble and diligent suitor to the throne of thy mercy.

Have mercy on all sinners, I beseech thee, dear Jesus; turn their vices into virtues, and making them sincere lovers of thee, and observers of thy law, conduct them to bliss in everlasting glory. For the sake of thy glorious name, Jesus, and through the merits of thy bitter passion, have mercy also on the souls in purgatory. O Blessed Trinity, one eternal God, have mercy on me. Our Father. Hail, Mary.

Jesus! *(repeated ten times)* grant me the grace truly to love thee, for thine infinite goodness and those excessive bounties I have received, or shall ever hope to receive, from thee. Let the recollection of thy benignity and patience conquer the malice and wretched propensity of my perverse nature. May the consideration of the many deliverances, frequent calls, and continual helps I have received from thee during the course of my life, make me blush at my ingratitude. Ah, what return dost thou require of me for all thy mercies, but that I love thee; and why dost thou require it? Because thou art my only good! Thou art, my dear Lord! the sole object of my life, and I will diligently keep thy commandments, because I truly love thee.

Have mercy on all sinners, I beseech thee, dear Jesus; turn their vices into virtues, and making them sincere lovers of thee, and observers of thy law, conduct them to bliss in everlasting glory. For the sake of thy glorious name, Jesus, and through the merits of thy bitter passion, have mercy also on the souls in purgatory. O Blessed Trinity, one eternal God, have mercy on me. Our Father. Hail, Mary.

THE NINTH PETITION

Jesus! *(repeated ten times)* grant me the grace always to remember my latter end, and the account I am to give in after death; that so my soul may be always well disposed, and ready to depart out of this life in thy grace and favour. At that important hour, by the powerful intercession of thy blessed Mother, the glorious assistance of St. Michael and my good Angel, rescue my poor soul, O Lord, from the snares of the enemy of my salvation. Remember then thy mercy, O dear Jesus! and hide not thy face from me, on account of my offences. Secure me against the terrors of that awful period, by causing me now to die daily to all earthly things, and to have my conversation continually in Heaven. Let the remembrance of thy death teach me to set a just value on life; and the memory of thy resurrection encourage me to descend cheerfully to the grave.

Have mercy on all sinners, I beseech thee, dear Jesus; turn their vices into virtues, and making them sincere lovers of thee, and observers of thy law, conduct them to bliss in everlasting glory. For the sake of thy glorious name, Jesus, and through the merits of thy bitter passion, have mercy also on the souls in purgatory. O Blessed Trinity, one eternal God, have mercy on me. Our Father. Hail, Mary.

THE TENTH PETITION

Jesus! *(repeated ten times)* send me my purgatory in this life, and thus prevent me from being tormented in the cleansing fire which awaits for those souls who have not been sufficiently purified in this world. Vouchsafe to grant me those merciful crosses and afflictions which thou seest necessary for weaning my affections from things here below. Suffer not my heart to find any repose but in sighing after thee, since no one can see thee who loves any thing which is not for thy sake. Too bitter, alas! will be the anguish of the soul that desires to be united to thee, and whose separation is retarded by the heavy chains of sin. Keep me then, O my Saviour, continually mortified in this world, that being purified thoroughly with the fire of thy love, I may pass from hence to the immediate possession of thee in everlasting glory.

Have mercy on all sinners, I beseech thee, dear Jesus; turn their vices into virtues, and making them sincere lovers of thee, and observers of thy law, conduct them to bliss in everlasting glory. For the sake of thy glorious name, Jesus, and through the merits of thy bitter passion, have mercy also on the souls in purgatory. O Blessed Trinity, one eternal God, have mercy on me. Our Father.

"The Lord Jesus Christ for our sakes, became obedient unto death, even the death of the cross." *Philippians 2:8*

Hear these petitions, O most merciful Saviour, and grant me the grace frequently to repeat and consider them, that they may serve as so many easy steps, whereby my soul may ascend to thy knowledge and love, and to a diligent performance of my duty to thee and my neighbour, through the whole course of my life. Amen. Our Father. Hail, Mary. I believe in God.

THIRD PART

"At the name of Jesus let every knee bend, both in heaven, on earth, and under the earth; and let every tongue acknowledge that the Lord Jesus Christ is in the glory of God the Father." *Philippians 2:10 – 11*

Jesus! *(repeated ten times)* grant me grace to avoid bad company; or, if I should chance to come in the midst of such, preserve me being infected with the least temptation to mortal sin, through the merits of thine uncorrupt conversation among sinners. Art thou not always present, O Lord? and wilt thou not take an exact account of all our words and actions, and judge us accordingly? How then dare I converse with liars, slanderers, drunkards, or blasphemers; or with such whose discourse is either vain, quarrelsome, or dissolute. Repress in me, dear Jesus! every inordinate affection to carnal pleasures, or allurements to sensuality; and strengthen me by thy grace, to avoid such company as would enkindle the flames of those unruly appetites. May thy power, thy wisdom, and thy fatherly compassion, defend, direct, and chastise me; and cause me to lead such a life here amongst men, as may qualify me hereafter for the conversation of Angels.

Have mercy on all sinners, I beseech thee, dear Jesus; turn their vices into virtues, and making them sincere lovers of thee, and observers of thy law, conduct them to bliss in everlasting glory. For the sake of thy glorious name, Jesus, and through the merits of thy bitter passion, have mercy also on the souls in purgatory. O Blessed Trinity, one eternal God, have mercy on me. Our Father. Hail, Mary.

Jesus! *(repeated ten times)* grant me the grace to call on thee for help in all my necessities, and frequently to remember thy death and resurrection. Wilt thou be deaf to my cries, who hast laid down thy life for my ransom? or canst thou not save me, who took it up again for my crown? "Call on me in the day of trouble, and I will deliver thee." Whom have I in Heaven, but thee, O my Jesus! from whose blessed mouth issued such balmy words? Thou art my sure rock of defence against all mine enemies, and my gracious assistant in every good work. I will then invoke thee with confidence in all trials and afflictions, and when thou hearest me, O Jesus! thou wilt have mercy on me.

Have mercy on all sinners, I beseech thee, dear Jesus; turn their vices into virtues, and making them sincere lovers of thee, and observers of thy law, conduct them to bliss in everlasting glory. For the sake of thy glorious name, Jesus, and through the merits of thy bitter passion, have mercy also on the souls in purgatory. O Blessed Trinity, one eternal God, have mercy on me. Our Father. Hail, Mary.

THE THIRTEENTH PETITION

Jesus! *(repeated ten times)* enable me to persevere in a virtuous life, and never to grow weary in thy service till thou rewardest me in thy kingdom. In pious customs, holy duties, and in all honest and necessary employments, continue, O Lord, to strengthen me, both in soul and body. My life is nothing on earth but a pilgrimage towards the heavenly Jerusalem, to which he that sits down, or turns out of the way, can never arrive. May I always, O Jesus! follow thy blessed example. With how much pain, and how little pleasure, didst thou press on to a bitter death, that being the assured way to a glorious resurrection. Let me frequently meditate on those severe words of thine. "He only that perseveres to the end shall be saved."

Have mercy on all sinners, I beseech thee, dear Jesus; turn their vices into virtues, and making them sincere lovers of thee, and observers of thy law, conduct them to bliss in everlasting glory. For the sake of thy glorious name, Jesus, and through the merits of thy bitter passion, have mercy also on the souls in purgatory. O Blessed Trinity, one eternal God, have mercy on me. Our Father. Hail, Mary.

THE FOURTEENTH PETITION

Jesus! *(repeated ten times)* grant me grace to fix my mind on thee, especially whilst I converse with thee in time of prayer. Check the wanderings of my fanciful brain, put a stop to the desires of my fickle heart, and suppress the power of my spiritual enemies, who at that time endeavour to withdraw my mind from heavenly thoughts to vain imaginations. Thus shall I joyfully look on thee as my deliverer from all evil; and thank thee as my benefactor, for all the good I have received, or hope to obtain. I shall be convinced that thou art my chief good, and that all other things were ordained by thee only as the means to engage me to fix my affections on thee alone, that by persevering till death in thy love and service, I might be eternally happy. Let all my thoughts, O beloved of my soul! be absorbed in thee, that my eyes being shut to all vain and sinful objects, may become worthy to behold thee, face to face, in thy everlasting glory.

Have mercy on all sinners, I beseech thee, dear Jesus; turn their vices into virtues, and making them sincere lovers of thee, and observers of thy law, conduct them to bliss in everlasting glory. For the sake of thy glorious name, Jesus, and through the merits of thy bitter passion, have mercy also on the souls in purgatory. O Blessed Trinity, one eternal God, have mercy on me. Our Father. Hail, Mary.

THE FIFTEENTH PETITION

Jesus! *(repeated ten times)* grant me the grace to order my life with reference to my eternal welfare, sincerely attending, and wisely referring all the operations of my soul and body towards obtaining the reward of thy infinite bliss and eternal felicity. For what else is this world but a school for the tutoring of souls created for eternal happiness in the next? And how are they educated, but by an anxious desire of enjoying God, their only end? Break my froward spirit, O Jesus! by the reins of humility and obedience. Grant me grace to depart hence with the most sovereign contempt for this world, and with a heart overflowing with joy at the thoughts of going to thee. Let the memory of thy passion make me cheerfully undergo every temptation or suffering in this state of probation, for love of thee; whilst my soul, in the mean time, languishes after that life of consummate bliss and immortal glory, which thou has prepared for thy servants in heaven. O Jesus! let me frequently and attentively consider, that whatsoever I may gain, if I lose thee, all is lost, and that whatever I may lose, if I obtain thee, all is gained.

Have mercy on all sinners, I beseech thee, dear Jesus; turn their vices into virtues, and making them sincere lovers of thee, and observers of thy law, conduct them to bliss in everlasting glory. For the sake of thy glorious name, Jesus, and through the merits of thy bitter passion, have mercy also on the souls in purgatory. O Blessed Trinity, one eternal God, have mercy on me. Our Father.

"The Lord Jesus Christ for our sakes, became obedient unto
death, even the death of the cross." *Philippians 2:8*

Hear these petitions, O most merciful Saviour, and grant me the grace frequently to repeat and consider them, that they may serve as so many easy steps, whereby my soul may ascend to thy knowledge and love, and to a diligent performance of my duty to thee and my neighbour, through the whole course of my life. Amen. Our Father. Hail, Mary. I believe in God.

~

This text of the "Psalter of Jesus" is found in William A. Gahan, OSA, ed.,
The Christian's Guide to Heaven, or, A Complete Manual of Catholic Piety
(Dublin: T. M'Donnel, 1804), pp. 81 – 92 of the second section; and (Agra: Agra Press, 1834), Supplement, pp. 92 – 105. Gahan was born in 1730 and died in 1804.

The "Psalter of Jesus" is a very old Christian prayer, composed probably by Richard Whytford, a priest and a member of the order of Brigittines at Syon House, Middlesex, near London, in the fifteenth century. Bishop Richard Challoner (1691 – 1781), vicar apostolic of the London district, slightly modified Whytford's prayer, and it is Challoner's version that generally appears in eighteenth- and nineteenth-century prayerbooks.

The reverence intended in the "Psalter of Jesus" evoked a certain flexibility in praying it. One early nineteenth-century prayerbook says of the Our Father and Hail Mary at the end of each petition and of the Creed at the end of each Part: "These may be either retained, or omitted, according to each one's feelings or devotion." Another prayerbook says: "The holy Name is not to be repeated hastily, but with great reverence and devotion."

THE THIRTY DAYS' PRAYER TO OUR BLESSED REDEEMER, IN HONOUR OF HIS BITTER PASSION

For deliverance from any evil, or for obtaining some especial Mercy

~

O MERCIFUL Jesus, my blessed Saviour and Redeemer, the sweet comforter of all sad, desolate, and distressed souls; behold thy poor servant, humbly prostrate at the foot of thy holy cross, bewailing my misery, imploring thy mercy, and beseeching thee to take pity and compassion upon me in this my present affliction.

Hear my prayers, O assured refuge of the afflicted! behold my tears, consider my sorrows, and remedy my distresses; for, finding myself encompassed with very grievous calamities, by reason of my sins, I know not whither to fly for succour, or to whom I may make my complaint, but to thee, my meek and merciful Saviour, with a full hope and confidence that thou wilt vouchsafe thy accustomed pity to my humble petition. This I humbly entreat of thee.

By the holy mystery of thy alliance with our human nature, when, resolving with the Father and the Holy Ghost to unite thy divine person to mortal flesh for man's salvation, thou didst send thy angel to the holy Virgin Mary with those happy tidings, and clothing thyself with our human nature, remainedst, true God and true man, for the space of nine months in her sacred womb.

By the anguish thou enduredst when, the time of thy designed passion drawing nigh, thou prayedst to thy eternal Father, that if it were possible that bitter chalice might pass away from thee; yet concluding with a most perfect act of resignation, "Not my will, but thine be done."

By the outrageous injuries, shameful disgraces, cruel blows, contumelious blasphemies, forged witnesses, false accusations, and unjust judgments, which thou, innocent Lamb! patiently enduredst; by the shackles which fettered thy limbs, the tears which flowed from thine eyes, the blood which trickled from thy whole body; by the fears, sorrows, and sadness of thy heart; by the shame thou receivedst in being stript of thy garments, to hang naked on the cross, in the sight of thy sorrowful Mother, and in the presence of all the people.

By thy royal head crowned with thorns, and smitten with a reed; by thy thirst quenched with vinegar and gall; by thy side opened with a spear, whence issued blood and water, to refresh our souls with that living fountain of thy love and mercy; by the sharp nails wherewith thy tender hands and feet were cruelly pierced and fastened to the cross; by the recommendation of thy departing soul to thy heavenly Father, saying, "Into thy hands I commend my spirit"; by thy praying for thy enemies, "Father, forgive them, for they know not what they do"; by thy giving up the ghost, when thou criedst out with a loud voice, "My God, my God, why hast thou forsaken me?" and then, bowing down thy most blessed head, saidst, "It is consummated."

By the great mercy thou shewedst towards the penitent thief, saying, "This day thou shalt be with me in Paradise"; by thy descent into Limbus, and the joy thou communicatedst to the just souls therein detained; by the glory of thy triumphant resurrection, and the consoling appearance thou frequently didst vouchsafe for forty days' space to thy sacred Virgin Mother, to thy apostles, and thy other chosen friends and servants; by thy admirable ascension, when, in the sight of thy holy Mother and thy Apostles, thou wast elevated into heaven; by the miraculous coming down of the Holy Ghost in the form of fiery tongues, whereby thou replenishedst the hearts of thy disciples with thy love, and gavest them strength and courage to plant thy faith in the whole world; by the dreadful day of general judgment, on which thou wilt pass sentence on all mankind.

By all those sorrows, joys, passions, compassions, and whatsoever else is dear to thee in heaven and on earth, take pity on me, O compassionate Redeemer! hear my prayers, and grant me that for which I now most humbly and heartily petition thee. (*Mention here your request, or reflect mentally upon it.*)

Give me, O gracious Saviour, speedily to experience thy divine succour and comfort, who, according to the accustomed sweetness of thy tender heart, art wont to grant the requests of those who fear and love thee, even to their soul's desire and satisfaction; bestow on me also, O blessed Jesus, a constant faith, a firm hope, a perfect charity, a true contrition, a sincere confession, a full satisfaction, a diligent guarding of myself from future failings, a contempt of the world, a complete conquest of my passions, a zealous imitation of thy exemplary life and conversation, an entire accomplishment of my vows, an absolute mortification of my self-will, a willing readiness to die for thy love and honour, a final perseverance in grace and good works, a happy departure of my soul out of this world, with my perfect senses about me, and with thy holy sacraments to strengthen me; thyself, O dear Jesus, to comfort me! thy sacred Virgin Mother, with the saints, my particular patrons, to pray for me; and my good angel to conduct me to eternal rest and happiness. Amen.

This "Thirty Days' Prayer to Our Blessed Redeemer" is found in The Poor Man's Manual of Devotions; or, Devout Christian's Daily Companion *(Dublin: D. Wogan, 1819), pp. 56–61; in* The Golden Manual; or, Guide to Catholic Devotion, Public and Private *(London: Burns & Lambert, 1850), pp. 438–40; and in other nineteenth-century prayerbooks available in Ireland and England. The text above is that in* The Golden Manual. *However, the many versions of this prayer differ only slightly.*

THE THIRTY DAYS' PRAYER
TO THE BLESSED VIRGIN MARY,
IN HONOUR OF THE SACRED PASSION
OF OUR LORD JESUS CHRIST

By the devout recital of this prayer, for the above space of time, we may confidently hope to obtain our lawful request. It is particularly recommended as a proper devotion for every day in Lent, and all the Fridays throughout the year.

~

EVER-GLORIOUS AND blessed Mary, queen of virgins, mother of mercy, the hope and comfort of dejected and desolate souls; through that sword of sorrow which pierced thy tender heart, whilst thine only Son Jesus Christ our Lord suffered death and ignominy on the cross; through that filial tenderness and pure love he had for thee, grieving in thy grief, whilst from his cross he recommended thee to the care and protection of his beloved disciple St. John; take pity, I beseech thee, on my poverty and necessities; have compassion on my anxieties and cares; assist and comfort me in all my infirmities and miseries, of what kind soever.

Thou art the mother of mercies, the sweet comforter and only refuge of the needy and the orphan, of the desolate and afflicted. Cast, therefore, an eye of pity on a poor child of Eve, and hear my prayer; for since, in just punishment of my sins, I find myself encompassed by a multitude of evils, and oppressed with much anguish of spirit, whither can I fly for more secure shelter, O amiable mother of my Lord and Saviour Jesus Christ! than to the wings of thy maternal protection? Attend, therefore, I beseech thee, with an ear of pity and compassion to my humble and earnest request.

I ask it through the mercy of thy dear Son: through that love and condescension wherewith he embraced our nature, when, in compliance with the divine will, thou gavest thy consent; and whom, after the expiration of nine months, thou broughtest forth from thy chaste womb to visit this world, and bless it with his presence. I ask it through that anguish of mind wherewith thy beloved Son, our dear Saviour, was overwhelmed on the Mount of Olives, when he besought his eternal Father to remove from him, if possible, the bitter chalice of his passion. I ask it through the threefold repetition of his prayer in the garden, from whence afterwards, with sorrowing steps, and mournful tears, thou didst accompany him to the doleful theatre of his death and sufferings. I ask it through the wounds and sores of his virginal flesh, occasioned by the cords and whips wherewith he was bound and scourged, when stripped of his seamless garment, for which his executioners afterwards cast lots. I ask it through the scoffs and ignominies wherewith he was insulted; the false accusations and unjust sentence by which he was condemned to death, and which he bore with heavenly patience. I ask it through his bitter tears and bloody sweat, his silence and resignation, his sadness and grief of heart. I ask it through the blood which trickled from his royal and sacred head, when struck with his sceptre of a reed, and pierced with his crown of thorns.

I ask it through the excruciating torments he suffered, when his hands and feet were fastened with heavy nails to the cross. I ask it through his vehement thirst, and bitter portion of vinegar and gall. I ask it through his dereliction on the cross, when he exclaimed: "My God! My God! why hast thou forsaken me?" I ask it through his mercy extended to the good thief, and through his recommendation of his precious soul and spirit into the hands of his eternal Father before he expired, saying, "It is finished." I ask it through the blood mixed with water which issued from his sacred side when pierced with a lance, from whence a plenteous stream of grace and mercy has flowed to us. I ask it through his immaculate life, his bitter passion, and igno-minious death on the cross, at which nature itself was thrown into convulsions, by the bursting of rocks, rending of the veil of the temple, the earthquake, and darkness of the sun and moon. I ask it through his descent into hell, where he comforted the saints of the old law with his presence, and led captivity captive.

I ask it through his glorious victory over death, when he rose again to life on the third day, and through the joy which his appearance, for forty days after, gave to thee, his blessed Mother, his apostles, and the rest of his disciples, when, in thine and their presence, he miraculously ascended into heaven. I ask it through the grace of the Holy Ghost, infused into the hearts of the apostles, when he descended upon them in the form of fiery tongues, which inspired them with zeal for the conversion of the world, when they went forth to preach the gospel. I ask it through the awful appearance of thy Son, at the last dreadful day, when he shall come to judge the living and the dead, and the world by fire. I ask it through the compassion he bore thee in this life, and the ineffable joy thou didst feel at thine assumption into heaven, where thou art eternally absorbed in the sweet contemplation of his divine perfections.

O glorious and ever-blessed Virgin! comfort the heart of thy suppliant, by obtaining for me *(here mention your request, under the condition of its being agreeable to the will of God)*. And as I am persuaded my divine Saviour doth honour thee as his beloved Mother, to whom he can refuse nothing, so let me speedily experience the efficacy of thy powerful intercession, according to the tenderness of thy maternal affection, and his filial loving heart, who mercifully granteth the requests and complieth with the desires of those that love and fear him.

Wherefore, O most blessed Virgin, besides the object of my present petition, and whatever else I may stand in need of, obtain for me also of thy dear Son, our Lord and our God, a lively faith, a firm hope, a perfect charity, a true contrition of heart, unfeigned tears of compunction, a sincere confession, an abstinence from sin, a love of God and my neighbour, a contempt of the world, and patience under all affronts and ignominies; nay, even, if necessary, an opprobrious death itself, for the love of my Saviour Jesus Christ.

Obtain likewise for me, O sacred Mother of God! perseverance in good works, the performance of good resolutions, the mortification of self-will, a pious conversation through life, and, at my last moments, a strong and sincere repentance, accompanied by such a lively and attentive presence of mind as may enable me to receive the last sacraments of the Church worthily, and die in thy friendship and favour. Lastly, obtain, I beseech thee, for the souls of my parents, brethren, relations and benefactors, both living and dead, life everlasting. Amen.

~

This "Thirty Days' Prayer to the Blessed Virgin Mary" is found in William A. Gahan, OSA, ed., The Christian's Guide to Heaven, or, A Complete Manual of Catholic Piety, *Fourteenth Edition (Dublin: T. M'Donnel, 1804), pp. 127–31 of the second section; and in a later edition of this book (Agra: Agra Press, 1834), Supplement, pp. 148–52. The particular text used here is in* The Golden Manual, *pp. 441–44.*

O MY God, I believe in thee; do thou strengthen my faith. All my hopes are in thee; do thou secure them. I love thee with my whole heart; teach me to love thee daily more and more. I am sorry that I have offended thee; do thou increase my sorrow.

I adore thee as my first beginning. I aspire after thee as my last end. I give thee thanks as my constant benefactor. I call upon thee as my sovereign protector.

Vouchsafe, O my God, to conduct me by thy wisdom, to restrain me by thy justice, to comfort me by thy mercy, to defend me by thy power.

To thee I desire to consecrate all my thoughts, words, actions, and sufferings; that henceforward I may think of thee, speak of thee, willingly refer all my actions to thy greater glory, and suffer willingly whatever thou shalt appoint.

Lord, I desire that in all things thy will may be done, because it is thy will, and in the manner thou willest.

I beg of thee to enlighten my understanding, to inflame my will, to purify my body, and to sanctify my soul.

Give me strength, O my God, to expiate my offences, to overcome my temptations, to subdue my passions, and to acquire the virtues proper for my state.

Fill my heart with a tender affection for thy goodness, a hatred for my faults, a love for my neighbour, and a contempt for the world.

Let me always remember to be submissive to my superiors, condescending to my inferiors, faithful to my friends, and charitable to my enemies.

Assist me to overcome sensuality by mortification, avarice by alms-deeds, anger by meekness, and tepidity by devotion.

O my God, make me prudent in my undertakings, courageous in dangers, patient in afflictions, and humble in prosperity.

Grant that I may ever be attentive at my prayers, temperate at my meals, diligent in my employments, and constant in my resolutions.

Let my conscience be ever upright and pure, my exterior modest, my conversation edifying, and my comportment regular.

Assist me, that I may continually labour to overcome nature, to correspond with thy grace, to keep thy commandments, and to work out my salvation.

Discover to me, O my God, the nothingness of this world, the greatness of heaven, the shortness of time, and the length of eternity.

Grant that I may prepare for death; that I may fear thy judgments; that I may escape hell; and in the end obtain heaven, through the merits of our Lord Jesus Christ. Amen.

~

This "Universal Prayer," composed by Clement XI during his papacy (1700–1721), is found in William A. Gahan, OSA, ed. The Christian's Guide to Heaven, or, A Complete Manual of Catholic Piety, *Fourteenth Edition (Dublin: T. M'Donnel, 1804), pp. 263–64, and in a later edition (Agra: Agra Press, 1834), First Part, pp. 257–59.*